MARTIN LUTHER KING

Young Martin did not understand. Why was his friend Warren not at the same school with him? He soon learned the answer. Warren was white, and Martin was black – and that meant different schools and different futures in the USA of the 1930s.

But as Martin grew up, he began to dream of a better future for black people – a future in which black people had better jobs, better schools, and could vote. And he wanted to change things peacefully, without bombs and deaths.

In 1964, Martin Luther King became the youngest person, the first black, and the second American to win the Nobel Peace Prize. He had made an extraordinary journey – but death was not far away . . .

OXFORD BOOKWORMS LIBRARY
Factfiles

Martin Luther King

Stage 3 (1000 headwords)

Factfiles Series Editor: Christine Lindop

ALAN C. McLEAN

Martin Luther King

OXFORD UNIVERSITY PRESS

OXFORD
UNIVERSITY PRESS

Great Clarendon Street, Oxford OX2 6DP

Oxford University Press is a department of the University of Oxford.
It furthers the University's objective of excellence in research, scholarship,
and education by publishing worldwide in

Oxford New York

Auckland Cape Town Dar es Salaam Hong Kong Karachi
Kuala Lumpur Madrid Melbourne Mexico City Nairobi
New Delhi Shanghai Taipei Toronto

With offices in

Argentina Austria Brazil Chile Czech Republic France Greece
Guatemala Hungary Italy Japan Poland Portugal Singapore
South Korea Switzerland Thailand Turkey Ukraine Vietnam

OXFORD and OXFORD ENGLISH are registered trade marks of
Oxford University Press in the UK and in certain other countries

© Oxford University Press 2008

ISBN: 978 0 19 423393 4

A complete recording of this Bookworms edition of
Martin Luther King is available.

Printed in China

Word count (main text): 9,871

For more information about the Oxford Bookworms Library,
visit www.oup.com/elt/gradedreaders

Illustration page 2 by Gareth Riddiford

The publishers would like to thank the following for permission to reproduce images:
Alamy Images p 17 (Martin Luther & Coretta King/Charles Moore/Black Star); Art Archive p 7 (slave
ship); Associated Press p 20;Camera Press p 29; Corbis pp 12 (Joe Lewis & Max Schmeling/Bettmann),
14, 19 (Rosa Parks trial/Bettmann), 21, 35, 36, 37, 39 (President Johnson/Bettmann), 41 (The Black
Panthers/Bettmann), 45 (Bronx ghetto/JP Laffont/Sygma), 46 (Vietnam/Bettmann), 48 (anti-war
protest/Bettmann), 53 (Coretta Scott King at funeral/Bettmann); Getty Images pp viii(Martin Luther
King/Francis Miller/Time Life Pictures), 8 (slave poster/Hulton Archive), 9 (L'Ouverture/Hulton
Archive), 10 (Lincoln/Williamsburg), 11 (Ku Klux Klan/Keystone/Hulton Archive), 16 (Mohandas
K.Gandhi/Time Life Pictures), 25 (Minnijean Brown/A.Y Owen/Time Life Pictures), 27 (desegregation
demonstration/Truman Moore/Time Life Pictures); Magnum Photos pp 3 (segregated water/Elliott
Erwitt), 34; PA Photos p 23 (segregated students/WPS/AP), 44 (Mohammed Ali & Malcolm X/AP), 50
(looters/AP), 54 (Rosa Parks/Joe Marquette/AP), 55 (Condoleezza Rice/Pablo Martinez Monsivais/AP);
Redferns p 43; Topham Picturepoint pp 31, 32, 51.

CONTENTS

1   The man from Alabama

In 1963 a black minister from a small town in Alabama in the South of the United States led a march of more than 250,000 people to Washington DC. There he made a speech that became famous. 'I have a dream,' he said. He dreamed of all the people of America, black and white, living together in peace and freedom. He said that all men and women should be equal. Many of the marchers cried as they listened to him. The minister's speech was shown on television all over the world, and he became a hero to millions of people who saw and heard the speech.

But there were also people who hated this man and his ideas. They did not want black people to be free. They did not want them to have equal rights. In 1968, less than five years after his famous speech, a white man shot him dead. The minister was only thirty-nine years old. When people heard of his death, there was much sadness, and people cried in the streets. But many people were very angry too, and there were riots in the big cities. In Chicago and Washington black people burned buildings and fought the police. Hundreds of black people were killed in these riots.

Fifteen years after his death, the government of the United States made his birthday a holiday. Today he is remembered as one of the greatest Americans of the twentieth century.

Who was this man? Why did so many people love him? Why did others hate him?

The man from Alabama, the man who had a dream, was Martin Luther King. And the story of his life is the story of a people's fight for freedom.

Places in the Martin Luther King story

2 Growing up in the South

Martin Luther King was born on 15 January 1929 in Atlanta, Georgia. His father, who was also called Martin Luther King, was the minister in an Atlanta church. The King family were not poor. They lived in a good neighbourhood of Atlanta and they had enough money to live comfortably. When Martin thought about his early years in Atlanta, he remembered a loving family and friendly neighbours.

But the King family were black. Less than a hundred years before Martin Luther King was born, his people were slaves. Even in 1929 black people in the South of the United States did not have the same rights as white people. Blacks and whites lived in different worlds. When blacks travelled on buses, they had to sit at the back of the bus. They could not sit beside whites. Most restaurants did not sell food to black people. There were different schools for black children and white children. It was like this all over the South. Blacks and whites lived in the same places, but they were kept away from each other. This was called segregation.

'Segregation is wrong, but things will get better in time,' said Martin's father. 'White people will start to think differently one day. We should be patient and wait, because you can't hurry change. It will come, but not soon. We have to wait for it.'

Segregation

Young Martin did not agree with his father. 'If you want to change things, you have to act,' he thought. He knew himself what segregation meant. When he was very small, he played with a little white boy across the street from his house. His friend's name was Warren. When Martin started school, he looked for Warren, but he was not there. After school he went to Warren's house and asked to play with him. The boy's mother said that Martin could not play with Warren any more, because Martin was black and his friend was white.

When Martin came home that day, he was crying. He told his mother what had happened. 'It doesn't matter what other people think,' she told him, 'you're as good as anyone else. Don't you ever forget that!'

Martin remembered his mother's words. He knew that she was right. He was as good as any white boy. But as he grew older, he saw how white people treated black people in Atlanta.

Once when he was in the centre of town, he walked into a white woman. It was an accident, but the white woman hit him on the face. When someone asked her why she had done this, the woman replied, 'That little black bastard stepped on my foot.' Martin's face hurt, but the name that she called him – 'little black bastard' – hurt him even more.

When he started high school at the age of eleven, Martin began to make speeches. Of course, he often spoke in church, but at school he talked about the need for change in the South. When Martin was fourteen years old, he won a prize for one of his speeches. He travelled to Washington with his teacher to get his prize, and they returned to Atlanta by bus. When a white man got on the bus, there were no empty seats, so the driver told Martin to get up and give the white man his seat. Martin refused. Why should he give his seat to this man? The bus driver became angry and called him bad names. Finally, Martin gave the white man his seat because he did not want to make trouble for his teacher. But he was angry. It was not fair that he had to stand while a white man sat in his seat. He did not want to hate white people, but sometimes it was hard *not* to hate them.

3 Slavery and the South

In 1929 when Martin Luther King was born in Atlanta, Georgia, most black people in America lived in the South. In fact, nine out of every ten African-Americans lived in the South. In every way their lives were worse than the lives of Southern whites. They were poorer, they lived in worse houses, their lives were shorter. Most blacks in the South could not vote. Some black people who were alive in 1929 had been slaves. They had belonged to their white owners, and they were treated like things, not people. White people could buy and sell slaves just like houses or land.

In the past many countries have used slaves. Hundreds of years ago there were slaves in Rome and Athens. They worked on farms and in the houses of rich people, but they were not slaves for ever. After some years, they became free men and women again.

But in North and South America slavery was different. In the sixteenth century people from European countries like Britain, Spain, and Portugal began to move into North and South America. They cut down forests and cleared the land for farms. They needed men and women to work on their farms. Where could they find them? The answer was Africa.

Men and women were taken from their homes in Africa and brought to North and South America to work on farms and on roads. From about 1500 to 1850, European ships took at least 10 million men and women from Africa to become slaves in the Americas. The ships were very full, and the men and women did not have enough food, water, or air. Hundreds of thousands of Africans never reached America: they died on these slave ships.

When African slaves arrived in America, they were sold to white farmers. Often people from the same family were sold to different owners and never saw each other again. Husbands lost their wives, and children were taken away from their mothers. In the South of the United States the farms were very big. The farmers usually grew sugar or cotton, and they needed slaves to do the hard work in the fields. The white farmers gave the slaves food, clothes, and houses, but the slaves had to stay on the farm. They belonged to the farmer. When slaves ran away, they were usually caught and brought back to their owners. Then they were beaten and sometimes even killed.

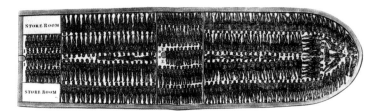

A slave ship

$1200
TO
1250 DOLLARS!
FOR NEGROES!!

THE undersigned wishes to purchase a large lot of NEGROES for the New Orleans market. I will pay $1200 to $1250 for No. 1 young men, and $850 to $1000 for No. 1 young women. In fact I will pay more for likely

NEGROES,

Than any other trader in Kentucky. My office is adjoining the Broadway Hotel, on Broadway, Lexington, Ky., where I or my Agent can always be found.

WM. F. TALBOTT.

Slaves were sold to white farmers

Many slaves fought against the slave-owners. In 1791 a black slave called Toussaint L'Ouverture led an army of slaves against French soldiers on the island of Haiti. Toussaint died in a French prison, but in 1804 Haiti became the first free black country. In Virginia in 1831, a slave called Nat Turner led slaves against their white owners. They did not succeed and Turner himself was killed, but the slave-owners were afraid that one day the slaves would win the fight.

Some black leaders wanted to return to Africa. In 1822 a new country was born in West Africa. This was Liberia, a country for people who were once slaves but were now free.

A hundred years later African-American leaders such as W. E. B. Dubois argued for a return to Africa.

After 1808 it was against the law to bring slaves from Africa to the United States. But the number of slaves in the South continued to grow. By 1860 there were more than 4 million slaves in the South. They were no longer Africans but African-Americans. And they wanted to be free.

Toussaint L'Ouverture

When Americans wrote the Declaration of Independence in 1776, they said that men and women should be free and equal. But the men who wrote the Declaration owned slaves. How was this possible? This was a difficult question. By the nineteenth century many black people had become Christians. They went to church on Sunday, just like their white owners. Blacks and whites both read the Bible. And the message of the Bible was the same: all men and women, black or white, are equal in God's eyes.

More and more people in Europe and America thought that slavery was wrong. Britain ended the buying and selling of slaves in 1807. A year later America did the same. Many Northern states ended slavery, and they wanted it to stop all over the United States. But Southern slave owners wanted to keep their slaves. They refused to free them, and they were ready to fight for their right to own slaves. The Southern states were ready to go to war for these rights.

4   War in America – and after

Abraham Lincoln was elected President of the United States in 1860. He wanted to end slavery in America, but the South wanted to keep their slaves. So seven Southern states decided to leave the United States of America.

The North and South went to war in 1861. More than 180,000 black soldiers fought for the North. In five years of terrible fighting, more than half a million soldiers on both sides were killed. The North won the war and slavery in the South ended in 1865.

Abraham Lincoln

Now there were no more black slaves in America. But black people in the South did not have the same rights as white people. Blacks could not go to white schools and there were very few schools for blacks. Blacks could not go to the same shops or restaurants as whites. When blacks did try to get their rights, whites often answered them with violence.

Most whites in the South were angry that they had lost the war. They did not agree with the end of slavery or with equal rights for

The Ku Klux Klan

blacks. In 1867 a group of soldiers in the Southern state of Georgia started a secret organization to fight against black rights. This organization was called the Ku Klux Klan. They wanted to frighten blacks and stop them from voting in elections. Klansmen dressed in white clothes and covered their faces, so nobody could see who they were. Sometimes they took black people out of their homes and beat them or killed them. They also burned the schools, homes, and churches of black people. In the 1890s more than 1,000 blacks were killed by whites in the South. Most blacks were too frightened to tell the police because many policemen in the South actually belonged to the Klan. Early in the twentieth century more than 4 million whites belonged to the Ku Klux Klan.

Now that blacks were not slaves, they were free to move out of the South. Thousands of blacks left the South and moved to Northern cities like Chicago and Detroit. There was more freedom for blacks in the North and there was work for them in the factories. By the beginning of the twentieth century a quarter of blacks lived outside the South, mostly in big Northern cities.

In the twentieth century, blacks began to play a more important part in the life of America. New schools and universities for blacks opened. Jazz, the music of black people, became popular all over the world. Harlem, a black neighbourhood of New York City, became the centre for black musicians like Duke Ellington and black writers like Langston Hughes. Paul Robeson was a famous black singer and actor. He sang about the troubles of black people. But

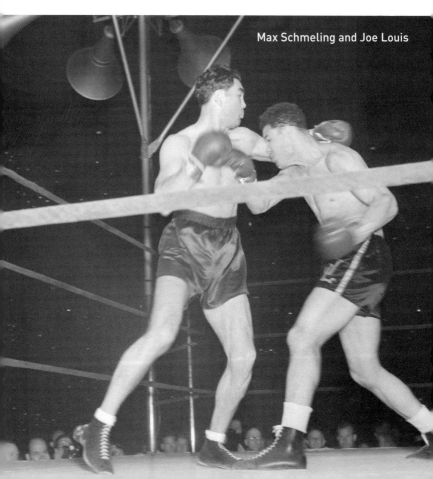

Max Schmeling and Joe Louis

many whites were angry when he appeared in Shakespeare's play *Othello* with a white actress as his wife.

There were many black sportsmen. The great black runner, Jesse Owens, won gold medals for America at the 1936 Olympic Games in Berlin. As Hitler and other Nazi leaders watched, Owens beat the best white runners. The boxer Joe Louis was born into a poor black family in Alabama in 1914 and was taken to Detroit when he was ten years old. In 1937 he became the world boxing champion. His greatest fight was against the German boxer, Max Schmeling. Louis had lost to Schmeling in their first fight. When Schmeling returned to Germany he was called a hero by the Nazis. Hitler himself said that because Schmeling had won, whites were stronger than blacks. When Louis beat Schmeling in 1938, blacks all over America were wildly happy. Joe Louis fought twenty times as world champion and was never beaten.

But once again the greatest changes in the lives of black people came from a war. In 1941 America entered the Second World War. Black soldiers fought bravely for their country, but the American army was segregated. Black soldiers did not fight beside white soldiers and they were not treated as well as white soldiers. When black soldiers protested about this, there were often fights between black soldiers and white soldiers.

When these black soldiers returned to America, they wanted equal rights for themselves. In some of the countries they had visited, black people had the same rights as white people and were treated fairly. After the war even more blacks moved to the North and became richer. Some things got better: black workers in 1950 were paid twice as much as black workers in 1940, and more blacks began to go to university. But black Americans got much less money than white Americans – even when they were doing the same jobs. Many fewer blacks than whites went to university. And even in the North there was still the problem of racism.

The Second World War had been a war against racist ideas. Many whites in America realized that their own country was racist. Blacks began to vote and white politicians began to listen to them. In 1948 President Truman ended segregation in the army. In 1954 a new law said that blacks and whites must go to the same schools and learn together. Things were getting better for black people. But they wanted more. They were ready for someone to lead them towards greater freedom. They were ready for Martin Luther King.

Black soldiers in the Second World War

Learning

Martin Luther King was an excellent student. When he was only fifteen, he went to Morehouse College in Atlanta. He was a clever young man and he finished his studies there in 1948. Martin's father wanted him to be a minister, but at first Martin said no. He did not want to follow his father so soon. He was learning exciting new ideas from his teachers at Morehouse, and there was so much more that he wanted to know.

But slowly Martin began to think differently. He decided to become a minister like his father, but to be a teacher too. He went to Crozer, a college for ministers in Pennsylvania, in the North. There were many white students at the college, but Martin was happy to find that they were friendly towards him – in fact, they welcomed him. Martin realized that black people and white people did not have to hate each other. But how could he make white people in the South see this? He wanted to make them think like him, but he did not know how. He began to think seriously about this.

In his last year at Crozer, Martin went to hear a talk about the Indian leader, Mohandas Gandhi. Gandhi and his followers had fought against the British in India. But they had used non-violence, not guns, to get a free India. They had refused to pay money to the British government. They had sat in the road to stop the British army. Thousands of them had been arrested for refusing to obey unfair laws.

Mohandas Gandhi

Gandhi thought that love was more powerful than hate. 'If you love your enemies, you can beat them,' Gandhi had said. Martin was excited by Gandhi's words. Could black people in the South end segregation without violence?

Martin continued his studies at Boston University. Now he was Dr Martin Luther King. His family were very proud of him.

But Martin was lonely in the North. He felt far from home, and he knew that his work was in the South. Then some friends introduced him to a young woman from the South called Coretta Scott. They fell in love and married in 1953. Soon they started a family. For the rest of Martin Luther King's life, he and Coretta worked together to fight segregation in the South.

In 1954 the Kings moved back to the South. Martin became minister of the Dexter Avenue Baptist Church in Montgomery, Alabama.

Once he was back in Alabama, Martin realized that things were beginning to change in the South. Black and white children were starting to go to the same schools. There were new laws against segregation. But white people in the South decided to fight against these laws. Clearly, trouble was coming in the South. And the trouble began in Martin Luther King's new home – Montgomery, Alabama.

Coretta and Martin

6 The Montgomery bus boycott

Rosa Parks was a black woman who worked in a shop in Montgomery. Every day she took the bus to and from her work. One day in December 1955 Rosa Parks got on the bus to go home and sat in a seat at the front. There were three other black people sitting near her. More and more people got on the bus, and soon there were no more seats. White people had to stand. The driver stopped the bus and asked the black people at the front to give their seats to white people. Three of them stood up but Rosa Parks stayed in her seat.

Rosa belonged to the NAACP, a black civil rights group, and she knew her rights. She refused to get up.

'Why don't you stand up?' said the driver.

'I don't think I should have to stand up,' Rosa answered.

'If you don't stand up, I'm going to call the police,' said the driver.

'You can do that,' said Rosa.

So the driver called the police and Rosa Parks was arrested and put in prison.

The arrest of Rosa Parks made many black people in Montgomery very angry. But it gave them a chance to protest against the policy of segregation on the buses. For years the NAACP had wanted to take action against the city's bus company. Now they had a chance. But who could lead them? Martin Luther King had only been minister of the Dexter Avenue Baptist Church for a year, but he was well known for his honesty. The NAACP asked King to meet them and decide what to do. It was time to end segregation on Montgomery's buses.

They met in King's church. King said that black people should boycott the buses in Montgomery. 'If we refuse to ride on the buses, the company is going to lose a lot of money,' he said. 'In the end they will *have* to end segregation.' King agreed to lead the boycott.

When the meeting finished, King was worried. He discussed his worries with Coretta, his wife. 'Will the bus boycott succeed?' he wondered. 'Will black people obey the

Rosa Parks

Martin Luther King talks to reporters in Montgomery

boycott? Most black people don't have cars, so how are they going to get to work? If people can't get to work, perhaps they will lose their jobs. Maybe the boycott will hurt black people more than it will hurt white people. How will that help black people?' There were a lot of questions, and King and his wife talked for hours. Neither of them slept well that night.

Next morning King and Coretta got up and looked out the window. There was a bus stop in front of their house. They waited for a bus to come. At last the first bus came – and it was empty. Then the second bus came – and it was empty too! It was the same all over Montgomery. Black people walked to work – some of them walked twenty miles – or stayed at home. Black taxi drivers drove people to work in their taxis for the same money that they paid on the bus. The boycott was working!

The bus boycott lasted for more than a year. Many black people were arrested and put in prison, and King was one of them. Some white people were angry with King and they thought he was dangerous. One night someone left a bomb outside the King family home. It exploded, but luckily no one was hurt.

The bus company was losing money, but it refused to change its policy. Shops in Montgomery were losing money too because black people were not coming into town to shop. The owners of the shops wanted the boycott to end, but the bus company did not want the NAACP to win. The boycott leaders went to an Alabama judge. They said that segregation on buses was wrong. The Alabama judge did not agree with them, so they went to Washington to see the most important judges in the country. On 13 November 1956 these judges said that segregation in buses was against the law. The Montgomery bus boycott had succeeded!

King in prison

7 Big trouble in Little Rock

The Montgomery bus boycott made Martin Luther King famous. People all over America began to talk about the young black minister who had organized it. But King knew that Montgomery was only the beginning. Black people had won their fight in Montgomery, but it was not the only fight that they had to win in the South. To win their civil rights, black people needed to organize themselves.

In 1957 hundreds of Southern black church leaders met together to talk about what to do next. At the meeting King said that black people had to work together to win their civil rights. The church leaders organized themselves into the Southern Christian Leadership Conference (SCLC). Martin Luther King became the president of the SCLC. He told them that they had to join together to fight for the rights of black people in the South.

King wrote a book, *Stride Toward Freedom*, to explain his ideas. In his book, he talked about the teachings of Gandhi. King believed that non-violence was the only way to win the fight for black rights. In Montgomery, the boycott had been non-violent. The police had beaten the protesters, and they had tried to break the boycott by violence, but the protesters had not fought back. They had no sticks or guns, and they had not fought violence with violence.

They had just refused to let people treat them unfairly. And they had won because they were right, not because they were violent.

There were many other things in the South that needed to change. Schools were segregated: white children went to all-white schools, black children went to all-black schools. Although there were more black children than white children in the South, much more money was spent on white schools than on black schools.

But in 1954 the law was changed. Now it was against the law to have different schools for black children and white

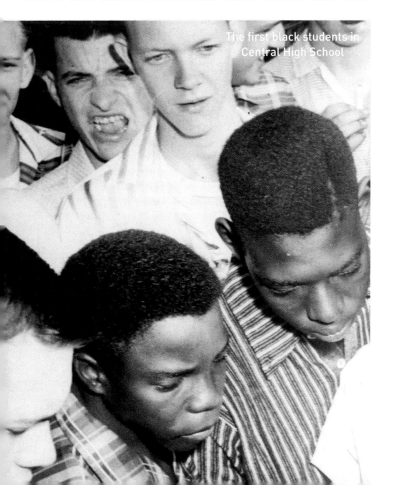

The first black students in Central High School

children. The new law said that all schools had to take both black children and white children.

Change came slowly to the South. Many white people hated the new law, and in many Southern states, they refused to obey it. Arkansas was one of these states. In the state capital, Little Rock, nine black students tried to enter the Central High School at the start of the 1957–58 school year. Little Rock soon became one of the most famous places in the story of the fight for civil rights.

On 2 September, the night before the start of the new school year, the leader of the Arkansas government, Orval Faubus, ordered the National Guard to stand outside Central High School. He told them to stop any black students from entering the school, because he was afraid of trouble from protesters. The school was closed. But a judge said that Faubus could not use the National Guard to do something that was against the law. On 23 September the Little Rock police took the nine black students into Central High. A crowd of more than a thousand white people tried to stop the black students from entering. The crowd rioted and attacked the police. The pictures of the riot were seen all over the world, and many Americans were shocked to see such ugly attacks in their own country. Next day, the President of the United States, Dwight D. Eisenhower, ordered the army to Little Rock. A thousand soldiers stood in front of the crowd as the nine black students entered Little Rock Central High School. Every morning the nine black children walked to the school, and every morning the soldiers protected them as they walked through crowds of angry whites.

One of the Little Rock Nine, Elizabeth Eckford, later talked about that walk past the angry crowd.

'I looked for a friendly face in the crowd. I saw a nice-looking old woman. She seemed to have a kind face. But when I smiled at her, she spat at me.'

Inside the school, things were different. Ernest Green, one of the nine black students, remembered the friendly white students who helped him. 'I missed three weeks of school, so I was behind in my class work. A couple of boys in my class gave me notes on the lessons that I'd missed. After seeing the crowd outside the school, I was really surprised by this.'

Soldiers protecting the Little Rock Nine

8   A new start?

For black people in America, 1960 was an important year. King was busier than ever. He decided to move back to his father's church in Atlanta. He spent half of his time working in his church and the other half working for the SCLC.

King's policy of non-violent protest was becoming more popular. Soon black people found a new way to protest – the 'sit-in'.

Restaurants in the South were still segregated. One day in February 1960 four black students in Greensboro, North Carolina, walked into a shop called Woolworth's. There were hundreds of Woolworth's shops across the country, and many had restaurants inside the shop. The students sat down at a table and politely asked for lunch. The waitress refused to take their order and told the students to go, but they refused to leave the restaurant. Instead, they began a sit-in: they sat at their tables and waited until the restaurant closed. Next day some more students joined them. Then some white students joined the sit-in too. The Greensboro students were arrested, but the sit-ins did not stop. Soon there were sit-ins at restaurants all over the South. More white students from the North travelled to the South to join the sit-ins. In July 1960 Woolworth's finally agreed to let both blacks and whites use their restaurants. Other big companies did the same. So once again, non-violent protest had been successful in the battle for civil rights.

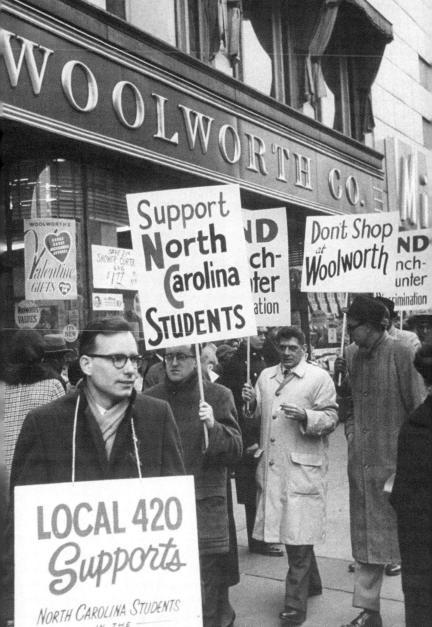

Outside Woolworth's, Greensboro, in 1960

Martin Luther King joined the sit-ins. When students held a sit-in at an Atlanta restaurant in October 1960, King stayed with them. He was arrested and put in prison.

King was not sorry to go to prison. Like Gandhi, he believed that you should not obey a bad law. If the law is unfair, he argued, then it is right to break it. It is better not to obey a bad law than to obey it. If this means that you go to prison, then you have to accept that.

King was not afraid of prison. But King's family and friends were afraid for him. They knew that King's life was in danger in prison. He had many enemies and there were people who wanted to kill him. In the South in 1960 it was not difficult to kill a black prisoner. Coretta King went to John F. Kennedy for help. Kennedy had already said that segregation was a bad thing, and he promised to help King. When Kennedy asked the judge to let King go, the judge agreed. But Martin Luther King later went to prison many more times when he refused to obey unfair laws.

One month later, in November 1960, John F. Kennedy became President of the United States. Across the country, people were full of hope. The young President promised a new start. Surely this must mean the end of bad laws, and freedom at last for black people in the South?

But most white people in the South still did not want change. They were ready to fight to keep their way of life. There was a road to freedom, but it was not short, and it was not easy.

John F. Kennedy becomes President

9 From Birmingham to Washington

1963 began badly for the SCLC and Martin Luther King. He had had success in Montgomery and Greensboro, but now, for the first time, he failed. The SCLC tried to end segregation in Albany, Georgia. They fought against the town government and the police for almost a year. But at the end of the year, Albany's schools, libraries, and parks were still segregated. King had lost in Albany. Now he needed to win somewhere. He started to think about Birmingham, Alabama.

Birmingham was one of the worst cities in the country for black people. It was sometimes called 'Bombingham', because there had been so many bomb attacks on houses and churches in black neighbourhoods. There had been eighteen of these attacks in the last six years, but no one was ever arrested for them. The chief of the Birmingham police was a man called Bull Connor. When the SCLC organised protests in Birmingham, Connor's policemen beat the protesters and attacked them with dogs. Hundreds of protesters were hurt, and hundreds were arrested. King was one of the protesters who went to prison.

When he was in prison, King read that some white church leaders had called for an end to the protests. They said it was not the right time for protests. King was angry when he read this. He wrote a letter to the white churchmen. In it he said:

'You say it is not the right time to protest. You say "Wait!" For years I have heard the word "Wait!" For too many years black people have waited. Too often "Wait!" means "Never!"'

There was a problem with the protest. When men and women were arrested and put in prison, they often lost their jobs. It was difficult for black families when their fathers and mothers were in prison. 'Why not ask young people to join the protest?' King said. Plenty of school children wanted to join the protesters in Birmingham, because they wanted to help. Freedom was as important to them as it was to their parents. Some black leaders were worried about this plan.

Birmingham, Alabama

'These young children will get hurt when the police attack,' they said. But King's reply was, 'Segregation will hurt them even more.'

On 2 May 1963, fifty children aged from six to eighteen marched to the centre of Birmingham. They were arrested and put into prison. Then another fifty did the same. They were also arrested and put in prison. Then another fifty, then another. By the end of the day a thousand children were in prison. Birmingham's prisons were full. At first the police were too surprised to do anything. But next day they came with police dogs and powerful water hoses. Men, women,

Using water hoses against protesters

and children were knocked down by the power of the water and attacked by the dogs.

When the protests were shown on television, the violence of the Birmingham police shocked many Americans. Black people were attacked by police just because they wanted the same rights as white people. People all over the country knew that this was not right. They knew that things had to change. And people in other countries were shocked too. How was this possible in a country like the United States of America, the 'land of the free'? People began to ask questions about freedom in America. Was it only for white Americans? What about black Americans?

Birmingham agreed to stop segregation in its schools and on its buses. King had won the battle. Later in the year he had his finest moment. In the summer of 1963, President Kennedy tried to get a new civil rights law. Civil rights leaders organised the biggest protest march of all to support the president. They wanted people from all over the country to go to Washington DC and ask for equal rights for black Americans.

On 28 August 1963, more than 250,000 people came to Washington and marched to the Lincoln Memorial. There were speeches and songs. Finally,

Martin Luther King stood up and made the greatest speech of his life. 'I have a dream,' he said. In the America of his dream, blacks and whites were equal and lived together in peace. The speech was shown on television all over the world. People cried when they heard King's words. Surely things must change now, they thought. The country was full of hope for the future.

But later in that year, 1963, America was once again shocked by terrible violence.

'I have a dream...'

10 'This country is sick!'

A month after King's Washington speech, there was more violence, again in Birmingham, Alabama. A bomb was thrown into a black church and four young black girls were killed. King's message did not change, but the bomb made it harder to persuade people that non-violence was the answer.

After the church bomb, Birmingham

On 22 November 1963, President John F. Kennedy was shot dead in Dallas, Texas. King had known Kennedy well and worked with him. They had argued about the best way to win equal rights for blacks, but they had agreed that equal rights for all must come soon.

Like most Americans, King was shocked by Kennedy's death. 'This country is sick!' he said. Sometimes he thought about his own death. Perhaps somebody hated King enough to kill him too.

He wondered about the new president. Lyndon B. Johnson came from the South. What was his policy on segregation – did he want to end it, like Kennedy, or to continue with it? Nobody knew the answer yet.

After his Washington speech King became famous all over the world. When people thought of the fight for civil rights in America, they thought of Martin Luther King. In 1964 he won the Nobel Peace Prize for his civil rights work. He was only thirty-five years old – the youngest person and only the second American ever to win this important prize. At the end of 1964 *Time* magazine named him 'Man of the Year'.

King's work continued. In the South very few black

leaders were elected to government. Before people could vote, they had to register. Very few blacks did this, because it was very difficult. In Mississippi, for example, only 7 per cent of blacks were registered to vote. King realized that he had to get blacks to register and then vote. That was the best way to change the segregation laws in the South.

Registering black voters was difficult in many states, but Alabama was one of the worst. More than 300,000 blacks in this state wanted to vote but were not registered. King was asked to help black voters to register in Selma, Alabama.

The march to Montgomery

Selma was a small town of 30,000 people. Half of the people in Selma were black but only 1 per cent of them were registered to vote. If blacks wanted to register to vote, they had to pass a reading test. Almost all failed the test, although they could often read better than the whites who gave them the test. To register, blacks had to go to an office that was only open twice a month. The white people who worked in the office arrived late and left early. When blacks tried to register, they were often told to go away.

King and the SCLC planned a protest march from Selma to Montgomery, 50 miles away. Montgomery was the state capital, and it was in this city that the arrest of Rosa Parks had started the battle for civil rights. The march started on 7 March. Police met the marchers on the road to Montgomery and told them to go back. When the marchers refused the police attacked them. They beat the protesters and one man was killed. Once again, people all over the world were shocked by police violence against peaceful protesters. President Lyndon B. Johnson ordered the Selma police to protect the marchers. On 21 March the march from Selma to Montgomery started again. It took five days, but this time there was no violence. When the march entered Montgomery, there were 25,000 marchers, black and white.

The leader of the Alabama government, George Wallace, refused to meet the marchers or listen to their protests. But the message of the marchers reached the government in Washington. Later that year, Martin Luther King was there when President Johnson signed the Civil Rights Law of 1964. This law protected the rights of all Americans to vote, and it was one of the most important laws of Martin Luther

King's life. It made a big difference to blacks in the South. In 1963 only 6 per cent of blacks in the South were registered to vote: by 1969, 66 per cent were registered. Now no one could stop blacks from voting for their own leaders.

President Lyndon B. Johnson with King, signing the Civil Rights Law

11 'I'm black and I'm proud!'

The 1960s were a time of great change in America. Young people all over America were asking questions about their country. They did not always believe what their parents believed. They wanted change. At the march on Washington a young singer called Bob Dylan put the thoughts of young Americans into his song *The Times They Are A-Changin'*. Things are changing fast, the song said. The old must listen to the young – and they cannot stop change.

Young blacks did not want to wait patiently for change. Although they knew that Martin Luther King had worked hard for equal rights, they thought that change was happening too slowly. They wanted power for black people and they did not want to ask politely for it. Perhaps violence was necessary for change, they thought.

In 1966 Bobby Seale and Huey Newton started the Black Panther Party. The Panthers did not agree with Martin Luther King about the use of non-violence. They said that blacks should buy guns to protect themselves from attacks by whites. Huey Newton said that the Civil Rights Law of 1964 was 'too little too late'. After a fight between the Panthers and the police, Newton was arrested and put into prison because he killed a white police officer. Crowds of Panther supporters marched through the streets, shouting

The Black Panthers

'Free Huey!' Other Panthers died in battles with the police. Most white Americans were afraid of the Black Panthers. They thought that they were violent criminals. But the Panthers also did some good work. They opened schools in poor black neighbourhoods and gave food and clothes to blacks. After a few years, the Black Panther Party broke into smaller groups. But its message reached many young African-Americans and made them proud to be black. They started to learn about Africa, eat African food, and wear African clothes.

Another person who wanted a different America for blacks was Malcolm X. In the past, many blacks had the name of their slave owner as their last name, so Malcolm changed his last name from Little to X. For him, it was a way of saying goodbye to slavery. Like the Black Panthers, Malcolm X did not agree with Martin Luther King about the use of violence. Blacks should not ask for help from whites, he thought; blacks should help themselves. Violence was necessary when you were fighting for your rights. Malcolm said that blacks should fight violence with violence – it was the only language that white racists understood. 'If a man speaks the language of violence,' said Malcolm, 'you can't speak to him in the language of peace. He'll break you in two. If a man speaks French, you can't speak to him in German. You have to find out what this man speaks. Once you know his language, learn how to speak his language. Then we can talk.'

Many young blacks agreed with Malcolm X more than with Martin Luther King. They were angry that they still did not have the same rights as whites. Poor blacks living in the big cities of the North wanted to vote, but they wanted other things too. They wanted better houses and more jobs. In many of the poorer neighbourhoods of America's big cities young blacks rioted. Many people died in these riots.

In the 60s, many important black writers and musicians became famous in America. Writers like James Baldwin and Toni Morrison showed Americans what the lives of black people were like. In his book *The Fire Next Time*, Baldwin warned of terrible violence in the future. To stop this, whites must change their ways, he said. The black musician Stevie Wonder sang about the difficulties of young blacks. One of his songs told the story of a young boy who was born in the South but moved to Chicago to find work. He finds that in the North he is free – but free only to be poor. Why was anyone surprised that young blacks were angry?

Perhaps the most famous black man in the 1960s was

Stevie Wonder

the boxer Muhammad Ali. Born Cassius Marcellus Clay in 1942 in Louisville, Kentucky, young Clay won an Olympic gold medal in 1960. He fought the world champion Sonny Liston in 1964 and, to the surprise of most people, Clay won. After the fight, he surprised the world when he said that he had become a Muslim and had changed his name to Muhammad Ali. 'Don't call me Cassius Clay,' he said. 'That's a slave name.' Ali was loud and proud and clever. 'I am the greatest', he said. And he was. No one could beat him.

He began to speak out against racism. In 1967 he refused to join the US Army and fight in Vietnam. Because of this he was put in prison and he was told that he was not the world champion any more. When he got out of prison, he beat George Foreman to become world champion again. Ali said, 'When I refused to fight in Vietnam, . . . I wasn't a hero. I just wanted to be free. I wanted America to be America.'

Malcolm X and Muhammad Ali

12 'Black and white, unite and fight!'

The late 1960s were a time of change for Martin Luther King too. Although he was always against violence, he began to see that there were many different kinds of violence. King was from the South and he wanted freedom and equal rights for the blacks of the South. But life for blacks in Northern cities was not easy either. Blacks in the North could go to

the same schools as whites, but many black children did not finish school. Most Northern blacks were poor. Many could not find a job when they left school. Many came from one-parent families and lived in buildings that were old and dirty.

American soldiers in Vietnam

It seemed to King that poverty was itself a kind of violence. He began to think about the rights that all people should have. It was true that black people had the vote, true that they could eat in the same restaurants as whites. But it is one thing to be able to eat in a restaurant; it is another thing to have the job that gives you the money to eat there. King believed that a few rich people had too much money and millions of poor people had too little. He wanted an end to poverty – and that meant that someone had to take money from the rich and give it to the poor. It was a strong message, and many people who supported King on civil rights were not sure about it. These new ideas seemed dangerous to many of his supporters.

King took his marches and protests to the great Northern city of Chicago. He wanted to show America how black people lived in the cities of the North. And he saw that it was not just black people in the big cities who were poor. There was poverty among whites too. King wanted to unite poor black and poor white people – to bring them together to end poverty. 'Black and white, unite and fight!' he said. He led marches through the streets of Chicago. Just as in the South, the marchers were attacked by the police. Sometimes it was worse than in the South. The marchers were hit with sticks and bottles.

Some black leaders did not agree with King. They thought that he should only speak for black people. Why should he speak for poor white people? Poor whites had their own leaders. But King had decided what he wanted to do. He planned to lead a Poor People's March on Washington.

And now everyone in America was thinking about a new problem: Vietnam.

All through the 1960s America was at war in Vietnam. Every year more and more American soldiers were sent to fight in Vietnam. By 1968 more than half a million American soldiers were fighting there. Many of these soldiers were black and came from poor families. In the end more than 58,000 American soldiers died in Vietnam.

Vietnam was a terrible war. More than two million soldiers from North and South Vietnam were killed. More than two million Vietnamese who were not soldiers were killed or hurt. Thousands of villages were destroyed and rice fields were burned.

Many Americans were against the war. They thought it was wrong for America to go to war with a small country like Vietnam. King agreed with them. He was worried about what his country was doing. He decided to speak out against the war. Some of his friends told him not to do this. They said the war was not his business. He should only talk about the problems of black people. But on 4 April 1967 King made an important speech about Vietnam. He said he could not be silent about the war any more. People had said that he should not speak about peace – he should only speak about civil rights. 'These people,' King said, 'do not know me. They do not know the world in which they live.' Then he attacked the US government. He said the war on Vietnam was wrong. The burning and the bombing had to stop. The killing of Vietnamese men, women, and children had to stop. 'I speak as a child of God and as a brother to the poor. I speak as an American. The Vietnamese too are my brothers and sisters. The American government must stop its violence against the Vietnamese people. War is not the answer.'

Martin Luther King was attacked for this speech. What did he know about Vietnam? Some newspapers said he was supporting the Vietnamese government when American soldiers were fighting and dying.

But protests against the war grew. All over America protesters fought with the police. University students who refused to join the army and fight in Vietnam rioted. At Kent State University, Ohio, four white students were shot dead by the National Guard. 'Now we know what it feels like to be black,' said one white student.

Vietnam protesters

13   Death in Memphis

Many people who wanted to change America began to ask questions about Martin Luther King's policy of non-violence. Was it possible to change things in America peacefully? The Black Panthers and the followers of Malcolm X did not think so. They thought that the only answer to white violence was black violence. One young black leader, H. Rap Brown, said that violence was 'as American as apple pie.' More and more young blacks agreed with him. There were riots in the black neighbourhoods of cities like Detroit, Chicago, and Los Angeles. Young blacks joined gangs to protect their neighbourhoods from the police and from gangs in other parts of the city. Gangs fought against each other. Guns were used and many young black men were killed.

These killings made King very sad. He hated to see young black men killing each other. He understood why young blacks were angry, but he still thought that violence was not the answer. He tried to persuade young blacks to stop fighting each other and instead start fighting the government that kept them in poverty. But few young people wanted to listen to him. They thought that Martin Luther King did not understand them. To them he was yesterday's man. He belonged to the past.

In 1968 King was tired. Speeches, marches, and protests had been his life for more than twelve years. He had won many battles. Black people were freer than they had been

when he began his fight for civil rights. But he knew that
there were many more battles to fight. Blacks were still
poorer and less successful at school than whites. There were
few blacks in important jobs. Young black people did not
remember the battles King had won. They wanted more
change, and they wanted it now.

In March 1968, a group of workers in the city of Memphis,
Tennessee, decided to stop work because they were badly
paid. Most of these men were black, and they worked hard
to keep the city clean. They asked Martin Luther King to
help them with their protest.

King agreed to march with them. The marchers wanted to
protest peacefully, and they sang and held hands. But gangs
of young blacks did not want to protest peacefully. They
attacked the march, broke shop windows and fought with
the police. A young man was killed in the fighting.

After the march, King talked to the gangs. He explained
what he was trying to do. He said that violence was not
the answer. They needed to hold a peaceful protest. That
was the only way that the workers could win. Some of the

A riot in Memphis, 1968

King at his hotel, Memphis

young men from the gangs argued with King. They said that times had changed and that peaceful protests did not work any more. Finally, King persuaded them to join him. The gangs agreed to join the workers on their next march. They promised not to use violence. The date for the next march was 5 April.

On 3 April, King came back to Memphis and made a speech. It was full of hope. 'I have been to the mountain top,' he said. 'I have seen the Promised Land. I may not get there with you. But we as a people will get to the Promised Land.'

On the next day, 4 April, King told his friends that he needed some air. He went out of his hotel room just after 6 o'clock in the evening. Suddenly there was the sound of a gun. His friends ran outside and found King lying on the ground. Someone had shot him. Jesse Jackson, one of King's young supporters, held him in his arms. An hour later Martin Luther King died in a Memphis hospital. He was thirty-nine years old.

14   Still dreaming

Martin Luther King's death shocked America. Black Americans could not believe that they had lost their leader. At first they were shocked, but soon they were angry. 'Go home and get your guns!' the Black Power leader Stokely Carmichael told a crowd in Washington DC. There were riots in all the big cities in the USA. The rioters fought the police. Forty-six blacks were killed in the riots that followed Dr King's death.

James Earl Ray, a white American, was arrested and went to prison for King's murder. But many people did not believe that Ray had acted alone. They thought that white politicians had paid him to kill King. Even Coretta King did not believe that Ray had killed her husband.

Martin Luther King's body lay in his father's church in Atlanta. Thousands of people came to say goodbye to the man who led the fight for civil rights. Later, King's body was taken to lie beside his grandparents. There, written on a stone, are the last words of his most famous speech:

Free at last. Free at last.
Thank God Almighty,
I'm free at last.

After his death many people wanted to remember Martin Luther King in some way. In 1980 Stevie Wonder wrote a song called *Happy Birthday*. The song said that King's birthday should be a holiday for all of the United States. In

Coretta at King's funeral

1983 a new law named the third Monday in January Martin Luther King Day, a new American holiday. On 20 January 1986, the first Martin Luther King Day, Stevie Wonder sang at a concert to give thanks for King's life. In the year 2000, all fifty states had a holiday on this day for the first time.

What happened to the other people in the Martin Luther King story?

Jesse Jackson, who was with King when he was killed, stood for election as President of the United States in 1984 and 1988. Later he worked for President Clinton, and he has visited many countries to work for peace.

Bobby Seale still works for civil rights, but does not believe in guns and violence any more.

Malcolm X was shot dead in February 1965, as he was giving a speech at a meeting.

Huey Newton came out of prison in 1970 and went to

live in Cuba. When he returned from Cuba he left the Black Panthers after some trouble over money. He was shot dead in 1989 in a gunfight over drugs.

James Earl Ray was sent to prison for ninety-nine years. He died in Nashville in 1998 at the age of seventy, still protesting that he had not killed Martin Luther King.

Rosa Parks left Montgomery and moved to Detroit. She continued working for civil rights. In 1990 she met Nelson Mandela just after he left prison, and Mandela said that he

Rosa Parks and President Clinton, 1998

often thought about her brave action while he was in prison. She was given the Presidential Medal of Freedom in 1998. She died on 25 October 2005, aged 93.

Coretta Scott King began the King Center in Atlanta, Georgia, to continue her husband's work. For the rest of her life she worked for peace and civil rights. She died on 31 January 2006. Four US Presidents went to her funeral: George W. Bush, his father George H. W. Bush, Jimmy Carter, and Bill Clinton. Now Dexter Scott King, son of Martin Luther King and Coretta Scott King, manages the King Center. Martin Luther King's body was moved to the King Center, and now Coretta's body is there beside his.

And Martin Luther King? What can we say about him today, more than forty years since his death? Has his dream of a fair and equal America come true?

There are more black Americans in important, powerful jobs than ever before. More than 300 American cities are governed by black leaders. On television there are many black reporters and newsreaders. In 2001 Colin Powell became the first African-American Secretary of State for Foreign Affairs. In 2005 Condoleezza Rice was chosen for the same job. At a meeting in African-American History Month, she talked about what Martin Luther King's ideas meant to her. 'Black Americans,

Condoleezza Rice at Coretta's funeral

African-Americans, have always believed in America, even in the darkest times. They believed in America when America didn't believe in them. Martin Luther King told America that it should be true to itself. And finally America did the right thing by African-Americans.'

But only 59 per cent of black Americans are registered to vote. And the black vote is important, most of all when America votes for its president. In the presidential election of 2004, when George Bush beat John Kerry, more than 90 per cent of African-Americans voted for Kerry.

Martin Luther King's dream has not yet come true. Blacks and whites are not yet equal. Look at the young Americans who go to prison, cannot find a job, or die in street violence. For every white person who finds himself in this group, there are five blacks.

'Being black in America is like wearing shoes that don't fit,' an African-American writer has said. 'You can get used to them, but they're not comfortable. That's the way it's always been. It's the way it always will be.'

The fight for civil rights in America has had many leaders. It has also had other people who worked quietly for that fight. Many of those people were not well known at the time and nobody remembers them now. But for more than ten years Martin Luther King was the voice of those people. He was a great speaker whose words could persuade people. During the bus boycott in Montgomery, one of King's followers said, 'Dr King, you have the words that we're thinking, but can't say.'

And that is why we still remember Martin Luther King today.

GLOSSARY

act to do something; *(n)* **action**

attack to start fighting or hurting somebody

bastard a name used to insult somebody

believe to think that something is right or true

boxer a person who fights with his hands wearing thick heavy gloves

boycott to refuse to buy or use something as a way of protesting

champion the best player in a sport

Christian following the teachings of Jesus Christ

elect to choose somebody to be a leader by voting for them; *(n)* **election**

equal having the same rights as other people

freedom not being a slave; being able to do or say what you want

funeral the time when a dead person is buried

gang a group of young people who spend time together and often make trouble or fight other groups

government a group of people who control a country

hose a long tube used for carrying water

judge the person in court who decides how to punish somebody

law all the rules of a country; a rule that says what you can or cannot do

lead to control a group of people; *(n)* **leader**

medal a piece of metal with words and pictures on it that you get for doing something very good

minister a priest in some Christian churches

Muslim a person who follows the religion of Islam

National Guard a part of the US army that can be used to help in an emergency

neighbourhood a part of a town or city

organize to plan something and make it happen; *(n)* **organization** a group of people who work together to do something

persuade to make somebody do something by talking to them

policy the plans of a government or organization

politician a person who works in politics

poverty being poor

power the ability to control people or things; *(adj)* **powerful**

prize something that you give to the person who wins a game, race etc

protect to keep somebody or something safe

protest *(n & v)* to say or show strongly that you do not like something

proud pleased about something that somebody has done

racism the belief that some groups of people are better than others; **racist** a person who thinks this

register *(v)* to put your name on an official list

right *(n)* what you are allowed to do by law; **civil rights** the right to vote, work, etc equal to everybody else

riot *(n & v)* when a group of people fight and make a lot of noise and trouble

shocked surprised and upset

slave a person who belongs to another person and must work for them for no money; *(n)* **slavery**

speech a talk that you give to a group of people

spit (past tense **spat**) to send liquid from your mouth

state a part of a country with its own government

support to say that somebody or something is right or the best

treat to behave in a certain way towards somebody; *(n)* **treatment**

violence behaving in a way that can hurt or kill people or damage things

vote to choose somebody in an election

war fighting between armies of different countries

Martin Luther King

ACTIVITIES

ACTIVITIES

Before Reading

1 **How much do you know about black people in America? Are these sentences true (T) or false (F)?**

1 The number of Africans who were taken to North and South America to become slaves was five million.
2 Slavery in America was ended in 1808.
3 Until 1948 black soldiers and white soldiers did not work together in the US Army.
4 Black children have always been able to go to the same schools as white children.
5 More than a quarter of all black American men will go to prison at some time.
6 Up to 2008 there has not been a black President of the United States.

2 **How many of these people have you heard of? Match the people with the descriptions.**

Mohandas Gandhi, John F. Kennedy, Abraham Lincoln, Rosa Parks, Coretta Scott

1 She refused to give up her seat on the bus to a white person.
2 He was the US President from 1960 to 1963.
3 He was an Indian leader who used non-violence.
4 He was the US President during the Civil War.
5 She married and worked with Martin Luther King.

ACTIVITIES

While Reading

Read Chapters 1 and 2. Circle the correct word in each sentence.

1 Martin Luther King was from *Alabama/Washington DC*.
2 He was killed in *1963/1968*.
3 In Atlanta the King family had a *comfortable/difficult* life.
4 Martin Luther King and his father *agreed/disagreed* about how to end segregation.
5 In Atlanta white people treated black people *well/badly*.
6 When Martin was *eleven/fourteen* years old, he won a prize for speaking.

Read Chapters 3 and 4. Choose the best question-words for these questions and then answer the questions.

How / What / Which / Who / Why

1 _____ did so many slaves die on the journey from Africa?
2 _____ happened to slaves when they arrived in America?
3 _____ work did slaves do, and what did they get for it?
4 _____ led slaves against their owners in Virginia?
5 _____ did some Southern states want to leave the USA?
6 _____ did black people move north after the Civil War?
7 _____ New York neighbourhood became a centre for black musicians and writers?
8 _____ was never beaten as world champion?
9 _____ did things change for black soldiers after the Second World War?

Read Chapters 5 and 6. Match the beginnings and the endings of these sentences.

1 At first Martin did not want to be a minister,...
2 When Martin went to Crozer College...
3 Gandhi's teachings showed Martin...
4 After Coretta married Martin...
5 Rosa Parks refused to give up her seat...
6 Martin and Coretta were worried...
7 People knew that the bus boycott was a success...

a because she knew her rights.
b they worked together against segregation.
c that black workers would not obey the bus boycott.
d he saw that white people and black people could live peacefully together.
e but later he decided to follow his father and be a teacher as well.
f when the judges in Washington said that segregation in buses was against the law.
g that people could use non-violence to change unfair laws.

Read Chapters 7 and 8 and decide if the sentences are true (T) or false (F). Change the false sentences into true ones.

1 After the boycott, dozens of school leaders came together to make the SCLC.
2 King wrote his book to tell people about getting their rights through non-violence.
3 When the law about schools changed, many people in the South welcomed it.
4 Nine black children walked into Little Rock Central High School every morning past crowds of angry soldiers.

5 White students in the high school helped the black students.

6 In the South black people could not eat in the same restaurants as white people.

7 When the Greensboro students were arrested, the sit-ins stopped.

8 After five months Woolworth's said that blacks and whites could use their cinemas.

9 King was not afraid of prison.

10 Black people were hopeful when John F. Kennedy became President.

Read Chapters 9 and 10, then circle *a*, *b*, or *c*.

1 White church leaders told the protesters to _____.
   a) attack   b) wait   c) sit down

2 King asked _____ to help the protest.
   a) children   b) teachers   c) soldiers

3 People went to Washington to support the _____.
   a) government   b) protesters   c) president

4 King thought that the US was _____.
   a) sick   b) wrong   c) unhappy

5 Many blacks did not register to vote because it was very _____.
   a) expensive   b) difficult   c)   frightening.

6 The _____ stopped the march from Selma to Montgomery.
   a) army   b) president   c) police

7 The new law in 1964 meant that blacks could vote in _____.
   a) all of the US   b) the South   c) Alabama

Read Chapter 11, then complete the sentences with the names of these people.

Bob Dylan / Huey Newton / Malcolm X / /Muhammad Ali / Stevie Wonder / Toni Morrison

1 ...believed in the use of violence.
2 ...was a famous black writer.
3 ...sang about the need for change.
4 ...sang about the problems of young blacks.
5 ...refused to fight in Vietnam.
6 ...started the Black Panthers.

Read Chapters 12, 13, and 14 and answer these questions.

1 Why did King take his protests to Chicago?
2 Why did King's friends not want him to speak out against the war in Vietnam?
3 How did King think of the people of Vietnam?
4 What happened when young blacks began to join gangs?
5 How did most young black people think of King in 1968?
6 Why did black gangs attack the protest in Memphis?
7 How was Martin Luther King killed?
8 How did the US government remember Martin Luther King?
9 What has changed for black people since King died?
10 Why was Martin Luther King so important to the fight for civil rights?

ACTIVITIES

After Reading

1 **Complete these two newspaper reports using the words below (one word for each gap) The two headlines also need one word from the list.**

crowds, difficult, enter, everybody, happy, North, ordered, protect, refused, riots, segregation, shocked, should, sit-ins, soldiers, students, succeed, travelled, walked, white

1 _____ DAY AT LITTLE ROCK

The eyes of America were once again on Little Rock this morning. After the _____ that _____ the country earlier in the week, President Eisenhower yesterday _____ the army to _____ the Little Rock Nine when they tried to _____ the school. And today a thousand _____ stood between the angry _____ and the nine young black _____ as they _____ to Little Rock High School.

2 _____ DAY AT GREENSBORO

Yesterday Woolworth's agreed to end _____ in their restaurants in the South. This news comes after weeks of _____ which began in Greensboro, North Carolina when a white waitress _____ to serve black students. Since then, dozens of students, both black and _____, have joined sit-ins in Southern restaurants. Some have even _____ from the _____ to do so. One student said today, 'This shows that non-violent protest can _____. From now on, restaurants everywhere _____ be open to _____.'

2 **Use the clues below to complete this crossword with words from the story. Then find the hidden name in the crossword.**

1 With the same rights as other people.
2 A noisy fight with a lot of people.
3 A group of young people who like to be together and who get into trouble with other groups.
4 To start fighting somebody.
5 Muhammad Ali was a famous one.
6 Someone who belongs to another person and is not free.
7 To plan something and make it happen.

1							
			2				
		3					
4							
			5				
			6				
7							

The hidden name is _____.
Now write a sentence about this person.

3 **You are going to make a film about Martin Luther King's life. Answer these questions about your film.**

1 Who are the main characters? Which actors would you choose to play these characters?
2 What music would you use in your film?
3 What would you call your film?
4 Many films about a famous person have a second title

that explains why the person is important (for example, *Alexander the Great: Ruler of the World*). Think of a good second title for your film.

You have a meeting with a company that is interested in your film. To persuade them to give you the money you need, describe your film in 25 words or less.

4 **Do you agree or disagree with these ideas? Explain why.**

1 If you think a law is unfair, you can break it.
2 If you want to change things, you have to act.
3 If you love your enemies, you can beat them.
4 Sometimes it is necessary to use violence to change things.
5 Without Martin Luther King, there would still be segregation in America today.
6 Today blacks and whites in America have equal rights.

5 **Find out some more information about one of these people, then give a talk to your class or make a poster about them.**

- Joe Louis
- Harriet Tubman
- Stevie Wonder
- Paul Robeson
- Condoleezza Rice

Here are some websites that can help you.

Slavery and the American Civil War:
    www.americanrevwar.homestead.com

The history of black Americans:
    www.africanamericans.com

Martin Luther King:
    www.thekingcenter.org

ABOUT THE AUTHOR

Alan C. McLean has worked in English language teaching for more than forty years. After teaching in Zambia, he joined the British Council and worked in Venezuela and Nepal. He then joined an international publishing house for whom he worked as an editor and author. He wrote a number of English coursebooks and readers and to date has published more than fifty books. He was the editor of a series of original stories for English language learners and contributed ten stories to the series. For OUP he has written *From the Heart* for the Dominoes series of graded readers and a three-book secondary school course, Win with English. He also teaches literature courses and works as a university examiner. He has published two books of poetry and plays.

Alan C. McLean was born in Scotland but has lived for many years in Essex, in England. He is keen on sport and likes running (he has run marathons in London, Paris, and Amsterdam), cycling, swimming in the sea, and playing golf. He is very fond of cooking and eating Italian food. His other great love is music and he is an enthusiastic pianist. His favourite composers are Bach, Janacek, and Chopin.

OXFORD BOOKWORMS LIBRARY

Classics • Crime & Mystery • Factfiles • Fantasy & Horror
Human Interest • Playscripts • Thriller & Adventure
True Stories • World Stories

The OXFORD BOOKWORMS LIBRARY provides enjoyable reading in English, with a wide range of classic and modern fiction, non-fiction, and plays. It includes original and adapted texts in seven carefully graded language stages, which take learners from beginner to advanced level. An overview is given on the next pages.

All Stage 1 titles are available as audio recordings, as well as over eighty other titles from Starter to Stage 6. All Starters and many titles at Stages 1 to 4 are specially recommended for younger learners. Every Bookworm is illustrated, and Starters and Factfiles have full-colour illustrations.

The OXFORD BOOKWORMS LIBRARY also offers extensive support. Each book contains an introduction to the story, notes about the author, a glossary, and activities. Additional resources include tests and worksheets, and answers for these and for the activities in the books. There is advice on running a class library, using audio recordings, and the many ways of using Oxford Bookworms in reading programmes. Resource materials are available on the website <www.oup.com/elt/gradedreaders>.

The *Oxford Bookworms Collection* is a series for advanced learners. It consists of volumes of short stories by well-known authors, both classic and modern. Texts are not abridged or adapted in any way, but carefully selected to be accessible to the advanced student.

You can find details and a full list of titles in the *Oxford Bookworms Library Catalogue* and *Oxford English Language Teaching Catalogues*, and on the website <www.oup.com/elt/gradedreaders>.

THE OXFORD BOOKWORMS LIBRARY
GRADING AND SAMPLE EXTRACTS

STARTER • 250 HEADWORDS

present simple – present continuous – imperative –
can/cannot, must – *going to* (future) – simple gerunds …

Her phone is ringing – but where is it?

Sally gets out of bed and looks in her bag. No phone. She looks under the bed. No phone. Then she looks behind the door. There is her phone. Sally picks up her phone and answers it. *Sally's Phone*

STAGE 1 • 400 HEADWORDS

… past simple – coordination with *and, but, or* –
subordination with *before, after, when, because, so* …

I knew him in Persia. He was a famous builder and I worked with him there. For a time I was his friend, but not for long. When he came to Paris, I came after him – I wanted to watch him. He was a very clever, very dangerous man. *The Phantom of the Opera*

STAGE 2 • 700 HEADWORDS

… present perfect – *will* (future) – *(don't) have to, must not, could* –
comparison of adjectives – simple *if* clauses – past continuous –
tag questions – *ask/tell* + infinitive …

While I was writing these words in my diary, I decided what to do. I must try to escape. I shall try to get down the wall outside. The window is high above the ground, but I have to try. I shall take some of the gold with me – if I escape, perhaps it will be helpful later. *Dracula*

STAGE 3 • 1000 HEADWORDS

... should, may – present perfect continuous – *used to* – past perfect
– causative – relative clauses – indirect statements ...

Of course, it was most important that no one should see
Colin, Mary, or Dickon entering the secret garden. So Colin
gave orders to the gardeners that they must all keep away
from that part of the garden in future. **The Secret Garden**

STAGE 4 • 1400 HEADWORDS

... past perfect continuous – passive (simple forms) –
would conditional clauses – indirect questions –
relatives with *where/when* – gerunds after prepositions/phrases ...

I was glad. Now Hyde could not show his face to the world
again. If he did, every honest man in London would be proud
to report him to the police. **Dr Jekyll and Mr Hyde**

STAGE 5 • 1800 HEADWORDS

... future continuous – future perfect –
passive (modals, continuous forms) –
would have conditional clauses – modals + perfect infinitive ...

If he had spoken Estella's name, I would have hit him. I was so
angry with him, and so depressed about my future, that I could
not eat the breakfast. Instead I went straight to the old house.
Great Expectations

STAGE 6 • 2500 HEADWORDS

... passive (infinitives, gerunds) – advanced modal meanings –
clauses of concession, condition

When I stepped up to the piano, I was confident. It was as if I
knew that the prodigy side of me really did exist. And when I
started to play, I was so caught up in how lovely I looked that
I didn't worry how I would sound. **The Joy Luck Club**

BOOKWORMS · FACTFILES · STAGE 3

The USA

ALISON BAXTER

Everybody knows about the United States. You can see its films, hear its music, and eat its food just about everywhere in the world. Cowboys, jazz, hamburgers, the Stars and Stripes – that's the United States.

But it's a country with many stories to tell. Stories of busy cities, and quiet, beautiful forests and parks. Stories of a country that fought against Britain, and then against itself, to make the United States of today. Stories of rich and poor, black and white, Native American and immigrant. And the story of what it is really like to be an American today . . .

BOOKWORMS · FACTFILES · STAGE 3

Australia and New Zealand

CHRISTINE LINDOP

What do you find in these two countries at the end of the world? One is an enormous island, where only twenty million people live – and the other is two long, narrow islands, with ten sheep for every person. One country has the biggest rock in all the world and a town where everybody lives under the ground; the other has a beach where you can sit beside the sea in a pool of hot water, and lakes that are bright yellow, green, and blue. Open this book and start your journey – to two countries where something strange, beautiful, or surprising waits around every corner.